THE MYTH-MAKERS

A few words on TV between two internationally known scientists lasted only 11 seconds. But it was enough to keep a century old myth alive.

One asked whether the other knew many religious scientists. The other said virtually none, but occasionally he met them and felt a bit embarrassed. They both smiled.

The impression left with viewers of that recent programme* was that scientists who believe in God are few and far between, and a bit strange. And so, once again, a piece of outdated nineteenth century folklore—the idea that science has disproved God—was fed to the public. No wonder that some people imagine that all scientists are atheists!

For reasons like this, the mass media must bear some blame. If a scientist attacks a central truth of Christianity, that is news and gets 'on the box', but if a scientist says something in line with Christian beliefs, that is not news. And so the public get a one-sided picture. The fact is that some of the greatest scientists in history have been believers in God, and the same is true today.

Mike Poole, an award-winning educator in science himself, questioned ten scientists whose work is internationally recognised, and yet have no problem believing in a Creator God...

* *Heart of the Matter,* 29th Sept. 1996.

Sir Robert's extremely distinguished career led to a CBE in 1972 and a Knighthood in 1983. He was the Founding Director of the Mullard Space Science Laboratory, University College London, and Professor of Astronomy at the Royal Institution of Great Britain.

PROFESSOR SIR ROBERT BOYD CBE, FRS

- Emeritus Professor of Physics, University College London
- Fellow of the Royal Society

1,000 TIMES MORE POWERFUL THAN THE SUN

During the War, I worked on the detection of hidden enemy ships and, when peace came, I studied the invisible electrified layers in the upper atmosphere. I devised techniques to investigate these layers which, by good fortune, were just what was needed when satellites became available. In 1962 I used those techniques in Ariel 1, the first British instrumented satellite, which carried detectors for the Sun's rays that affect these invisible layers.

Puzzling data had been reported which suggested non-solar sources of X-ray radiation existed in the universe. I proposed a search for X-ray 'stars' and started work on the first cosmic X-ray reflecting telescope. In the meantime, simple detectors on rockets found more strong sources and their identification became urgent. X-ray astronomy was born, and rapidly revolutionised our picture of the skies.

> **'I proposed a search for the totally unknown.'**

Unlike the unchanging constellations, X-ray 'stars' appeared and disappeared in weeks, some pulsated regularly, others flared intermittently. The brightest source radiated a thousand times more power in X-rays than the total power of our Sun. Many were associated with black holes or neutron stars, a hundred thousand times smaller than the Sun and knowable only from the dramatic effect of their huge gravitational fields.

As this unexpected story unfolded, I often thought back to 1959, when I first proposed a search for the totally unknown. As a Christian I worship an unseen God, knowable only from his dramatic effect in Christ, in history and in human lives, and I thought how getting to know him had changed my whole world-view.

Malcolm Jeeves is a leading experimental psychologist who has held Foundation Chairs of Psychology at Adelaide University, Australia and at St. Andrew's, Scotland, where he was also Vice-Principal. He has served as Chairman of the International Neuropsychological Symposium and as Editor-in-Chief of the inter-national science journal Neuropsychologia. His CBE was awarded for his services to psychology.

PROFESSOR MALCOLM JEEVES CBE, PRSE

MYSTERIES OF THE MIND

My specialised research area of neuropsychology is one of the most exciting and fastest growing parts of contemporary science. Neuropsychology holds out promise of bringing greater understanding of such distressing conditions as Alzheimer's disease and schizophrenia.

Every fresh advance in our scientific understanding seems to tighten the links between mind and brain. Such evidence naturally prompts me to reflect on what my Christian faith teaches about human nature, and what I understand about terms in the Bible such as mind, body, spirit, heart, soul and so on.

As a neuropsychologist, my predominant picture is of the human being as a psycho-physical unity, unbelievably complex and calling to be investigated simultaneously from several different perspectives. What I find exciting and encouraging is that for a century now Biblical scholars have also been telling us that we are essentially a unity. But the language of the Bible, so profound and at times poetic, tells us things about our nature that we can so easily miss if we try to turn it into a scientific textbook of psychology—things that we need to know as we strive to be faithful disciples of our Lord Jesus Christ.

In every generation there are fresh challenges to integrate our basic Christian beliefs with new evidence coming from the scientific enterprise. As I do so I return again and again to a fresh awareness of the amazing fact that the God who created and keeps in being all that there is, humbled himself so that in the Lord Jesus Christ I can meet him daily as my Lord, Saviour and Friend.

- President of the Royal Society of Edinburgh (Scotland's premier learned society)
- Honorary Research Professor, School of Psychology, St. Andrew's University

'Research in neuropsychology holds out promise of bringing fresh understanding of Alzheimer's disease and schizophrenia.'

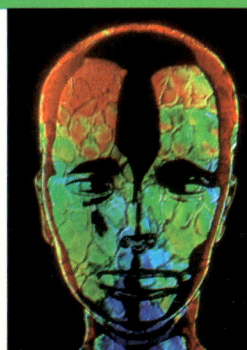

George Kinoti is chairman of the Kenyan government's Marine and Fisheries Research Institute, and was for many years head of Nairobi University's Zoology Department and Dean of Science. His London PhD is in parasitology.

In this piece, George explains that even though nature is no longer a 'Garden of Eden', he can still see evidence of the Creator's hand...

PROFESSOR GEORGE KINOTI

• Professor of Zoology, University of Nairobi, Kenya

'CLEVER' PARASITES

Parasites which cause major tropical diseases, such as malaria and bilharzia (schistosomiasis), are my field of study. They are particularly interesting organisms, able to survive in very hostile conditions.

For example, different parasites use very 'clever' stratagems for evading or overcoming the powerful defences of the human body. As a result, science is yet to develop an effective vaccine for any of these infections. The complexity of these apparently 'simple' organisms is such that no one parasitologist can master all that is known about any of them.

> 'We need both the scientific and Biblical understanding of ourselves and our world.'

The complexity, incredible ordering and beauty of the biological world speak, I am convinced, of a wise and powerful Creator. Like the heavens mentioned in the psalms of the Bible, the living world testifies eloquently to the Creator. Ignorance, prejudice or an irreligious culture can, however, make us deaf and blind to the beauty and meaning of creation.

Some years before entering college to study science I had become a Christian and was fully convinced of the truth of basic Christian beliefs. How was I to reconcile my Christian convictions with science?

In physics we learned that the physicists could not decide between the wave and the corpuscular theories of light and had to be content with both until better evidence became available. This helped me to see that the available evidence can lead to two quite different models of reality. Science and the Bible give us two different kinds of knowledge, or two models of the world, both of which are essential to our understanding of it. Many years of studying and teaching science have confirmed my initial conviction that we need both the scientific and Biblical understanding of ourselves and our world.

FIGHTING POVERTY WITH SCIENCE

Over the last ten years, George Kinoti has become increasingly interested in the use of science to overcome poverty. As we go to press, he is about to become Executive Director of the African Institute for Scientific Research and Development (AISRED).

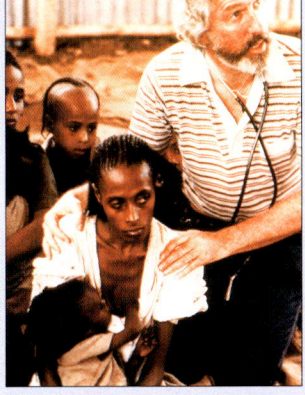

AISRED aims to use science to find effective solutions to the widespread problems of poverty and underdevelopment in Africa, as an expression of Christ's love to all people. It directs the talents and scientific expertise of Christians towards goal-oriented research and public education in the needy areas of agriculture, health, the environment, and the socio-economic field.

Leading Scientist Claims Young People Are Gullible

Richard Dawkins, TV scientist and author, has claimed that the persistence of religion is due to young people gullibly accepting their parents' beliefs. But this claim backfires. The persistence of many other beliefs—including atheism—could just as easily be put down to the upbringing of young people. The key issue is whether those beliefs are true or false, not how we came to believe them.

A student once criticised Dr Frederick Temple, then Archbishop of Canterbury, saying, 'you believe what you believe because of the way you were brought up.' Temple replied, 'That is as it may be. But the fact remains that you believe that I believe what I believe because of the way I was brought up, because of the way you were brought up'!

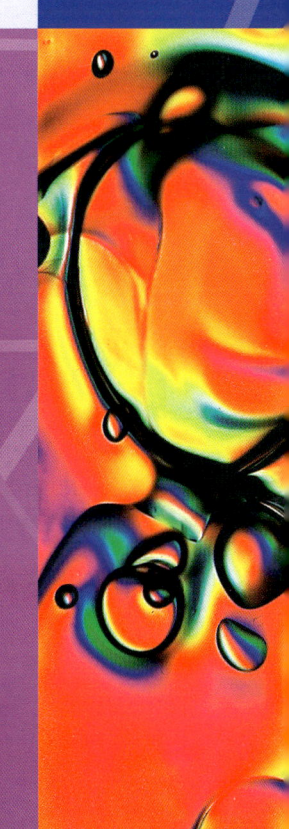

Gareth Jones' main areas of research are neurobiology and bioethics. Besides being Head of the Anatomy and Structural Biology Department, he is also Acting Director of the Bioethics Research Centre at the University of Otago. When does a foetus or embryo become a human being? That's the tough question Gareth is trying to answer...

PROFESSOR GARETH JONES

● Professor of Anatomy and Structural Biology, University of Otago, New Zealand.

WHEN DOES LIFE BEGIN?

Recently, I have investigated the question of whether, during early human development, one should attempt to identify a specific point when a 'brain' can first be recognised (brain birth, as opposed to brain death, which indicates the end of life). This is of considerable importance to society, because some people think that human embryos or foetuses prior to this point (whenever it may be) can be treated in a different fashion from those existing after this point.

This is one of a variety of topics I am researching that bring together all three of my commitments—science, ethics and Christianity. Throughout my career I have aimed to see science through Christian eyes. I have always been opposed to keeping the two separate. Christianity should influence everything I am, including my thinking and my integrity as a scientist.

I have deliberately made the human body the centre of my ethical interests, since I am an anatomist by training. This has plunged me into questions few others have tackled. Besides brain birth, another example is brain grafting (foetal neural transplantation)—the use of parts of the brains of aborted human foetuses for grafting into the brains of patients suffering from conditions like Parkinson's disease. Many object to this procedure because it involves aborted remains. My approach has been to assess whether this is a valid objection, partly by comparing this situation with our responses to other tragic medical situations where we aim to extract good from evil.

'This has plunged me into questions few others have tackled.'

The driving force for me is my Christianity and my commitment to ensure as far as possible that everyone (from foetuses to the aged) is treated with dignity. It's controversial territory, but my aim is to work out how Christian principles can best be applied in real life situations, when confronted by the possibilities of scientific and medical technology.

During a lifetime career in science, Sir John has been Professor of Atmospheric Physics at Oxford University, Director of the Appleton Laboratory, Chief Executive of the Meteorological Office and is a gold medallist of the Royal Meteorological Society and the Royal Astronomical Society.

SIR JOHN HOUGHTON CBE, FRS

'GARDENING' WITH GOD

I am both a scientist and a Christian and it has always been very important to me that the scientific and religious components of my life should fit together as two parts of a larger whole.

Many similarities exist in the way we think about science and religion; they are both searching for objective truth—truth about nature and truth about God. I agree with some of the great scientists in the early days of the scientific revolution 300 years ago who spoke of two books of God's revelation—the Book of Nature from which we learn about God's creative activity in the Universe, and the Book of God's Word, the Bible, from which we particularly learn of God's revelation of himself in Jesus. The views from these two books complement and support each other rather like the effect we experience when viewing through binoculars or through a stereoscope. A view with a single eye is flat, but with both eyes depth and perspective is added.

> 'Looking after the Earth is a responsibility given to humans by God.'

During recent years, my increasing involvement in the science of the environment has brought these two aspects of my life closer together. Looking after the Earth is a responsibility given to humans by God as described in the first chapter of the Bible. We were given the task of being 'gardeners' of the Earth and we have also been given the scientific and technical tools to help with the task. In our crowded, rapidly developing modern world, the task is enormously challenging. But we do not have to face it on our own; God offers us his partnership—a partnership which is tremendously exciting and which also provides real hope for the future.

- Chairman of the Royal Commission on Environmental Pollution
- Co-chairman of the Scientific Assessment for the Intergovernmental Panel on Climate Change
- Member of the Government Panel on Sustainable Development
- Fellow of the Royal Society

Owen Gingerich chaired the US National Committee for the International Astronomical Union and is councillor and former vice-president of the American Philosophical Society, America's oldest learned academy. He has also been awarded the Order of Merit from the People's Republic of Poland for his researches on Copernicus.

- Professor of Astronomy and the History of Science, Harvard University
- Senior Astronomer, Smithsonian Astrophysical Observatory, Cambridge, Massachusetts

PROFESSOR OWEN GINGERICH

FROM THE CORES OF ATOMS TO THE STAR-SPANGLED SKY

As a scientist, I accept scientific explanations as working hypotheses because they give a coherent, interlocking structure for our understanding of the universe. This intricately dovetailed system is vast in its panorama of space and time and astonishing in its range of analysis, from the cores of atoms to the molecular patterns of heredity to the star-spangled sky above. But science fails in discussing purpose and conscience. For me, the coherence of my total view of the universe includes a purposeful Creator who continues to act within Creation.

> 'Jesus Christ... direct evidence of God's interaction with the world.'

While we can see elements of deliberate intelligent design in the cosmos, the best we can do in looking at the natural world is to deduce a God of very large numbers. For a God of infinite love, a God who would be known to us, we must seek evidences of the divine through the inspiration of prophets through all ages and in many cultures. But for me, most especially, God's presence is revealed through the life and testimony of a particular person, Jesus Christ. Here a well-documented historical event gives direct evidence of God's interaction with the world.

Jesus' life of compassion, servanthood and forgiveness gives us hope on a grand scale, as we live our lives on this scientifically fascinating but strife-torn planetary home.

40% of Scientists Believe in God

A 1916 survey by James Leuba among 1,000 randomly selected scientists in the USA found that about 40% believed in a personal God. Leuba predicted that disbelief would increase with increasing education. 80 years on, Edward Larson and Larry Witham[1] repeated the 1916 survey as far as possible. They found that, even in this age of genetic engineering, about 40% of scientists still believe in a personal God and in an afterlife.

33,000 College Professors Professed Faith

The 1969 Carnegie Commission survey[2] of over 60,000 college professors in the USA showed that 55% of those involved in physical and life sciences described themselves as religious, and about 43% as attending church regularly. The 1996 Larson and Witham survey (see above) results suggest that if this 1969 survey were repeated today the figures would be similar.

Miracles and the Scientists

On 13 July 1984, fourteen Professors of Science in the UK, six of whom were Fellows of the Royal Society, signed a letter to The Times, saying, 'It is not logically valid to use science as an argument against miracles… We gladly accept the virgin birth, the Gospel miracles, and the resurrection of Christ as historical events.'

References: 1. *Nature*, Vol. 386, 3 April 1997, pp 435-6; 2. Stark, R. & Jannaccone, L. American *Economic Review: Papers and Proceedings, p. 436 (1996)*.

Professor Owen Gingerich by the 'Great 15 inch Refractor' of Harvard College Observatory.

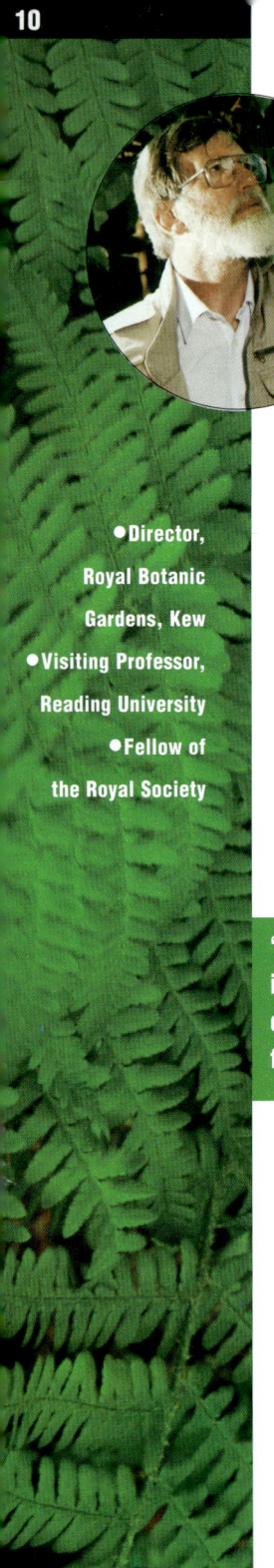

Sir Ghillean, who has around 50 plants named after him, spent 25 years leading botanical expeditions to unexplored areas of South America. He discovered hundreds of new species and helped the Brazilian government plan rainforest reserves. He has been awarded seven Honorary Doctorates by universities in the UK, USA, Sweden and Norway, won the International Cosmos Prize in 1993, and is a former Senior Vice-President of the New York Botanical Garden.

PROFESSOR SIR GHILLEAN PRANCE FRS

- Director, Royal Botanic Gardens, Kew
- Visiting Professor, Reading University
- Fellow of the Royal Society

THE DYING PLANET?

My scientific work has shown me much environmental destruction and that the environmental crisis faced by the world is serious. As I read the Bible, I find a great deal about creation and its ownership and stewardship. It clearly teaches that 'the earth is the Lord's and all that is in it.' I am concerned that the Church has been slow to react to the problem and I feel that I must use, to the best of my ability, the combination of my scientific knowledge and my love of the Biblical theology of creation to promote better care for our fragile planet by Christians and all people. The best motivated caretakers of our planet should be Christians, who know the Creator and have been saved by His Son, Jesus Christ.

> 'All my studies in science have confirmed my faith.'

For many years I have believed that God is the great designer behind all nature. I made a commitment to Christ as my personal Saviour while a student at Oxford University. All my studies in science since then have confirmed my faith. I regard the Bible as my principal source of authority.

During my career as a botanical explorer in the Amazon rainforest I have had many opportunities to support and affirm the work of missionaries and local churches in the region. I was constantly amazed at how many Brazilian Christians found it hard to believe that I am a scientist, because their only concept of foreigners was of missionaries. I feel I have been able to show many people that one can be both a scientist and a Christian.

Sam Berry studies the environmental and ecological factors leading to genetic changes in animals. He has been President of leading national and international bodies in his field, including the Linnean Society, the British Ecological Society, the European Ecological Federation and the Mammal Society.

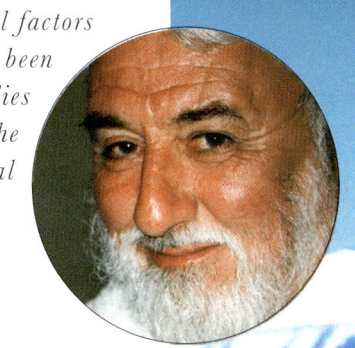

PROFESSOR R.J. (SAM) BERRY FRSE

SCIENCE IS THE STUDY OF GOD'S WORKS

My research has taken me to many wonderful places—Antarctica, the Andes, coral atolls, Atlantic islands—and more and more I am convinced that God has revealed himself in both creation and the Bible. It is a privilege and exciting as a scientist 'to think God's thoughts after him', in the words of Kepler. And as Calvin said, 'Being placed in this most delightful theatre, let us not decline to... delight in the clear and manifest works of God.'

Our scientific discoveries may force us to look again at our interpretations of particular Bible passages, but that is very different from questioning their authority as God's words. It is always worth remembering Galileo's words, who, after finding evidence that the Earth moves round the Sun, wrote that the Bible 'teaches us how to go to heaven, not how the heavens go'. We must be ruthless in seeking what God is trying to say through his word, and always be prepared to change our understanding.

I became a Christian in the year before I took science 'A' levels. My response to the explanation that Christ had taken upon himself the sins of the world, including my own, was a logical decision, based upon evidence in exactly the same way as I was being trained to gather scientific evidence and draw conclusions from facts and experiments. The correctness of that decision has been repeatedly confirmed for me both objectively (in terms of the consistency of Christian understanding of the world and God's account of it in the Bible) and subjectively (my experience of God working in my own life, including answering prayer).

Time after time, apparent conflicts between science and faith prove to be about our understanding of the Bible or nature, and not about God Himself.

> 'Time after time, apparent conflicts between science and faith prove to be about our understanding of the Bible or nature, and not about God Himself.'

• Professor of Genetics at University College, London

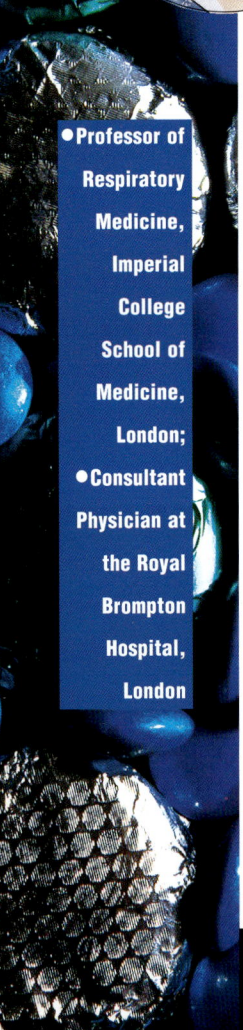

After medical school, Margaret Hodson specialised in respiratory medicine, taking a special interest in cystic fibrosis and lung transplantation. Today, besides working as a Professor and as a Consultant, she is Director of Medical Education at the Royal Brompton Hospital and Director of Postgraduate Studies (Heart & Lung Division) at the Imperial College School of Medicine. Margaret, in her daily work, faces the problem of human suffering, aware that it prevents many from believing in a loving God. Although there are no simple answers, she nevertheless sees light in the darkness...

PROFESSOR MARGARET HODSON FRCP

- Professor of Respiratory Medicine, Imperial College School of Medicine, London;
- Consultant Physician at the Royal Brompton Hospital, London

A CALLING TO MEDICINE

My chosen speciality brings me into contact with many young chronic sick. Some, in spite of the best possible medical care, will die young, and when a young person of 20 asks me, 'What is going to happen to me when I die?', it is a privilege and joy to explain that God loves him and that Jesus came to share the sufferings of this world and to win our salvation. I can explain simply that if we put our trust in Jesus then he will be with us for ever and has prepared a place in heaven for us. If I was not a Christian I would have no hope to give someone in that situation.

I was born to Christian parents and was taught about God and the Lord Jesus from an early age. When I was about 12 a Christian teacher took me to hear Billy Graham and I realised that I had to make my own decision to follow Jesus as my Lord and Saviour and could not just rely on my parents' faith. At 14, when I was quietly praying, God made it clear to me that I should study medicine. I have never doubted that call.

The birth, death and resurrection of Jesus Christ are essential points of Christian belief. As a Lay Reader in the Church of England, I have studied the evidence for the resurrection in great detail and find the evidence of the empty tomb, resurrection appearances, Christians' witness down the ages and my own personal experience of knowing Jesus absolutely compelling.

'I have studied the evidence for the resurrection of Christ in great detail and find it absolutely compelling.'

Faith & Science
—a Growing Interest

The popularity of science/faith studies is increasing. In fact, 'science and religion' has recently developed into an academic discipline in its own right. A look at *Who's Who in Science and Theology* gives an idea of the widespread interest. There are now several organisations for scientists who are Christians. In the UK the largest is probably Christians in Science, with about 1500 members and contacts. Its journal is *Science and Christian Belief*. In the USA, the American Scientific Affiliation has about 2,000 members and a journal, *Perspectives on Science and Christian Faith*.

Is Religion a 'Mental Virus'?

Viruses are nasty and they are catching. Critics of faith have called religion a 'mental virus'. This inevitably gives the impression that religion is a disease that should be avoided, but says absolutely nothing about whether it is true. It could just as easily be said that atheism is a mental virus too, spreading 'copy me' programmes from mind to mind.

Is God an Unnecessary Hypothesis?

If this means, 'Can you do science without bringing God in?', the answer is 'yes'. You can study jet engines without bringing in Frank Whittle. But if it implies that scientific explanations rule out God's activity, then the answer is 'no'. That's the mistake of the 'God-of-the-gaps' idea, which treats God like a stop-gap scientific explanation instead of the Creator of the whole show. Explanations of God's action are compatible with scientific explanations of how it all works.

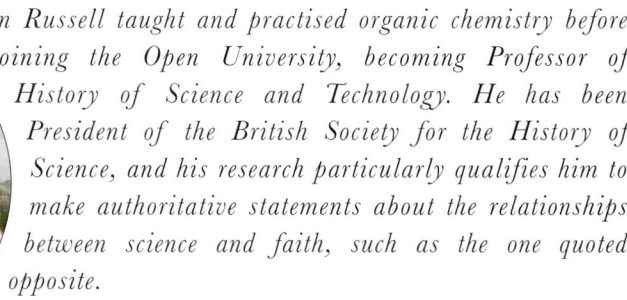

Colin Russell taught and practised organic chemistry before joining the Open University, becoming Professor of History of Science and Technology. He has been President of the British Society for the History of Science, and his research particularly qualifies him to make authoritative statements about the relationships between science and faith, such as the one quoted opposite.

- Fellow of the Royal Society of Chemistry
- Emeritus Professor of History of Science and Technology at the Open University
- Senior Member of Wolfson College, Cambridge

PROFESSOR COLIN RUSSELL, FRSC

THE LIGHT OF HISTORY

Even as a young scientist, the notion that the Bible and science were somehow in conflict struck me as laughable. That could only have been the case if one tried to pretend the Bible was a manual of scientific, as opposed to theological, truth.

A growing acquaintance with the history of science immensely strengthened this almost intuitive perception—here were multitudes of the most eminent figures in science whose world-views were rooted in Christ, for whom a 'conflict' with science was non-sensical, as recent historical studies have demonstrated. For them, as for me, the study of nature was a worthy vocation, positively encouraged by the Bible. This is splendidly illustrated by scientific history.

My own faith began as a teenager, after abandoning an early dislike of all things religious! It was one of life's turning points, and one which I have never had cause to regret. My faith began to mature at University, and even more so afterwards. As a scientist, I have always been concerned with questions of evidence, and of reasons for believing any given proposition. In living as a Christian, I soon saw that the authority I needed, the reasons for believing, lay in the Bible, the unique word of God. Experience of prayer, of worship and belonging to a Christian community have deepened that faith considerably.

'The notion that the Bible and science were somehow in conflict struck me as laughable.'

No Conflict

'To portray Christian and scientific doctrines as persistently in conflict is not only historically inaccurate, but actually a caricature so grotesque that what needs to be explained is how it could possibly have achieved any degree of respectability… The evidence points strongly in the direction of a myth… sustained by a campaign so well planned, so vigorous and so effective that even today, nearly a century later, the propaganda has lost little of its power… The Victorian scientific naturalists… in establishing their myth of an enduring conflict between religion and science… were successful beyond their wildest expectations.'*

Prof Colin Russell

*Abridged from 'The Conflict Metaphor and its Social Origins', *Science and Christian Belief*, vol. 1 no. 1 (1989), pp. 3-26.

Is Faith Childish?

Some people opposed to religion call belief in God primitive and childish, in order to contrast it with science as a mature, advanced way of thinking. When Jesus said we must become like little children, he meant we must learn to trust our Father God as a child trusts its parents, not throw our brains out!

Another strategy, intentional or not, is to criticise things that Christians don't actually believe. An example is to portray faith as anti-intellectual, as belief without evidence. This is the opposite of what Jesus taught—part of what he called the 'first and greatest commandment' was 'Love the Lord your God with… all your mind" (Matthew 22:37). Nor is faith a blind leap in the dark, but trust based upon evidence.

'"Taste and see that the Lord is good"… "Seek and you shall find"… The experimental approach is basic to Christianity.'
Professor Andrew Miller (Molecular Biologist)
Principal and Vice-Chancellor, University of Stirling

About the Author

'I became a Christian at the end of my second year as a physics undergraduate. I had to face the inevitable questions about how I could be both a Christian and a science student. Over 40 years I have carefully thought through the relationship of my commitment to Christ and my work in science education. When I became a university teacher I took up the study of the relationships between science and religion as my research area, with particular reference to education. I remain convinced that science and Christian faith are not enemies but allies. I have found many answers—and also many more questions! But that's what makes academic studies interesting and exciting.'

Mike Poole, author and compiler of 'God and the Scientists'.

Mike is a Visiting Research Fellow at King's College, University of London, winner of a Templeton Award for his MA module on Science and Religion, 1995, and a further award for his paper 'A Critique of Aspects of the Philosophy and Theology of Richard Dawkins.'*

*In *'The Poole-Dawkins Debate'*, available from Christians in Science, 5 Knockard Place, Pitlochry, Perthshire PH16 5JF. Price £1.00.

Further Information

If you would like to know more about the Christian faith and science, please contact the person who gave you this booklet, see the world wide web sites below and further reading list on the opposite page, or contact:

Christians in Science,
5 Knockard Place, Pitlochry, Perthshire, PH16 5JF, Scotland
or
The American Scientific Affiliation,
55 Market Street, MA. 01938-0668, USA.

Science and Faith on the Internet

Christians in Science
—http://www.tcp.co.uk/~carling/cis.html

Christian Students in Science
—http://www.totalweb.co.uk/csis

The American Scientific Affiliation
—http://asa.calvin.edu

FURTHER READING

MIKE POOLE:
'God and the Big Bang
—and the Science/Faith Debate',
CPO Design & Print (UK), 1996
—sample copy available for 50p from CPO
(see back cover for address);
'A Guide to Science and Belief'
(2nd ed.), Lion (UK) 1994.

SIR GHILLEAN PRANCE:
'Smart Plants',
CPO—Design and Print (UK) 1997
(orders: tel 01903 264556)
'The Earth Under Threat:
A Christian Perspective',
Wild Goose Pubns. (UK), 1996.

SAM BERRY:
'Real Science, Real Faith' (ed.),
Monarch (UK), 1995.

MALCOLM JEEVES:
'Human Nature at the Millennium—
Reflecting on the Integration of Pyschology
and Christianity',
IVP (UK)/Baker Book House (USA), 1997.

GEORGE KINOTI:
'Vision for a Bright Africa'
'Hope for Africa and
What the Christians Can Do'
both available from AISRED,
PO Box 14663, Westlands, Nairobi, Kenya.

SIR JOHN HOUGHTON:
'The Search for God: Can Science Help?',
Lion Publishing (UK), 1995.

GARETH JONES:
'Manufacturing Humans',
IVP (UK), 1987.

COLIN RUSSELL:
'Crosscurrents: Interactions between Science
and Faith',
2nd ed., Christian Impact (UK), 1995.

Professor R.J. (Sam) Berry FRSE

A CENTURY OF PROPAGANDA

Do top scientists reject the idea of God?

Has science finally removed the need for a God?

We often get the impression from the media that scientists are atheists, but as Mike Poole explains, the astounding reality is that the public have been misled for well over a century. Even in this age of cosmology, cyberspace and cloning, many scientists believe that faith and science should go hand-in-hand. In fact, the relationships between science and faith is one of the fastest growing and most controversial interests in the academic world today.

In this booklet, in non-technical language, ten international scientists tell of their fascinating work: some who have been involved in key discoveries and are now authorities on their subject; some who are at the leading edge of new areas of research. They also tell us about their belief in a Creator, and why their studies have not dented their faith, but strengthened it.

Prof R.J. (Sam) Berry FRSE
Prof Sir Robert Boyd CBE, FRS
Prof Owen Gingerich (USA)
Prof Margaret Hodson FRCP
Sir John Houghton CBE, FRS
Prof Malcolm Jeeves CBE, PRSE
Prof Gareth Jones (New Zealand)
Prof George Kinoti (Kenya)
Prof Sir Ghillean Prance FRS
Prof Colin Russell FRSC

ISBN 1-901796-02-7

CPO—Design & Print,
Garcia Estate,
Canterbury Road, Worthing,
West Sussex, BN13 1BW